Secrets of

Earning Money Without A Job!

How You Can Get $300 - $1,500 Within 30-Days!

Tashaya Singleton

Copyright © 2017 by Tashaya J. Singleton, Inc.

Also published as How To Get $300 - $1,500 Within 30-days

All rights reserved.

ISBN-10: 1545571545
ISBN-13: 978-1545571545

Dedication

To Brandon, Myles, Halo and Andrew, the youngest generation everything you need to succeed in life is already in you. Think, decide, believe and most importantly take action!

CONTENTS

	Acknowledgments	i
1	Facts About Earning and Jobs	1
2	The Basic Business Formula	4
3	How To Turn What You Know Into CASH	9
4	Fact of Earning: It Takes WORK!	14
5	Money Management Made Simple	21
6	Money Mindset Paradigm Shift	24
7	Choosing To Earn By Temping	30
8	The Earning Code Unlocked	33
9	Recommended Resources	36
10	Worksheets, Examples and Samples	38

Acknowledgements

I would like to thank all of the people that contributed to my lifelong experiential learning. Without all of you this book would not have been possible. My successes and my failures, especially the failures, have contributed to both my personal and professional growth and without them I would not be where I am today.

I applaud those of you that have purchased this book for your desire and effort to take control of your personal economy.

1 Facts About Earning And Jobs

If you are reading this book then you are in one of two positions:

1) You need money (or extra money)

2) You are ready to quit your job and start your own business

This book can help you, in either of the above positions. In these uncertain economic times we need to use what we already know to earn money. Long gone are the days of a lifetime career with one employer and the promise of a pension and gold watch for an employee's many years of loyal and dedicated service.

In this day and age the average person works for the same employer for 4.6 years and changes jobs 12 – 15 times in their lifetime according to the Bureau of Labor. And if you lose your job it could take anywhere from six months to two years for you to find a new one. Do you have enough in your savings account to cover your living expenses for two years, or even six months?

If you are one of the few people who have enough savings to maintain your current lifestyle, kudos to you. But, the majority of us just don't have that kind of money in our savings account. And don't feel bad, because the average American lives paycheck to paycheck and couldn't cover an emergency expense costing $500.00.

The Great Recession began in 2008, and yes lots of jobs were lost during this time. However, most of us have forgotten that there was intense downsizing in the 1980s. From 1992 – 1997 some 292 large companies downsized according to Compustat. In 2000 there was the dot-com bubble burst, and lots of jobs were lost during this time too. Jobs being eliminated and not returning has become the norm over the last few decades. To think something magical is going to happen and things are going to change is very wishful thinking. Now is the time to take control of your earning power. It is time to be resourceful because our jobs may have left us but our bills keep on coming, and the last time I checked utility companies and bill collectors don't take IOUs for payment.

Maybe you haven't been downsized and still have a job, but you're struggling to pay the bills each and every month. Or, possibly you don't feel you're getting paid what you are worth. You could be tired of long commuting and working hours. You may just want some extra money to pay for things you want, you know the latest and greatest gadget currently on the market. You could also be tired of being sick and tired, and ready to climb out of your current financial issues. Whatever your reason, this book is for you. It will help you earn $300 - $1,500 (or more) within 30-days, with a little bit of money, some time and a whole lot of effort using what you already know.

This is book isn't about a get rich quick plan, investment or money saving magic formula. It is a proven plan. Anyone with a positive mindset, a sincere desire, that doesn't mind putting in WORK and will follow the plan given in these pages can earn $300 - $1,500 or more within 30-days. And best of all, you can put this plan into action TODAY!

I know there are people who think that this can't be done because of their limited mindset, limited or no experience in earning money without a job. While writing this book I was asked if my process had been proven. I laughed as I assured people that this process has been proven many times. And, I am living proof that the plan in these pages works.

I have never held a job with the same employer for more than seven years. I have held **_way more_** than the average of 15 jobs in my lifetime. I have worked the following jobs:

Telemarketing:	cable television, magazines, telephone services, energy usage monitors, carpet cleaning services, catalog and infomercial products, websites, internet consulting services, appliance warranties, discount buyer's club membership, insurance, fundraising, alumni directories, surveys
Retail Sales:	clothing, furniture
Customer Service:	banking, insurance, appliance warranties, medical claims, patient account manager
Door-to-Door:	cutlery, telephone services, home improvement services
Receptionist	

Front Desk Clerk

Travel Agent

Marketing Research Assistant

And, there were probably more jobs that I just can't remember right now. Back then I was in the mindset, like most people, that I had to have a steady job with a reliable weekly or bi-weekly income to make sure the bills were paid. But somehow with all those jobs I still had times of unemployment, and underemployment, where the bills still had to be paid. During those times is when I used the information in these pages and earned the money I needed to my pay own bills.

2 The Basic Business Formula

There are really just five ingredients in this basic business formula:

1) Must be legal

2) Small Investment

3) $300 minimum return within 30-days

4) Start Today

5) Marketing, Promotion and SELLING

Yes, the dreaded word and task of SELLING is part of this plan. Selling is a basic requirement of **all** businesses. A business must SELL something to someone that has money in order to get money. If a business doesn't sell anything then it can't **_earn_** money.

Even service businesses and nonprofit organizations sell. A service business must convince people to buy the services that they offer in order for the business to get customers. A nonprofit organization must convince people that they serve a worthy cause in order to get donations from people.

We all know how to sell because it is part of our everyday life. Most people just don't realize that they are selling. If you are married you had to sell your spouse on why you were the person they should spend a lifetime with. You and your friends sell each other on which movie you all should go see or which restaurant you should eat at when you decide to spend time together. If you have or take care of kids you really sell on a regular basis. You have to convince them to eat their vegetables, clean their room, and go to bed at a certain time, among a multitude of other things.

All of the activities I just mentioned are a form of selling, you're just not getting paid cash money when you convince your family and friends to do them. So, now that we have a better understanding of what selling is, let us all stop dreading it and embrace it. Because no person or business can earn money without selling something.

The first requirement that a business be legal is self-explanatory. A small investment is required. The old saying *"it takes money to make money"* is still correct. But, it doesn't take as much money as you may think. Depending upon the skills you possess and the business that you choose, you could be in business today for about $25. The cost of business cards or flyers.

Starting your business **today** can be done as a Sole Proprietorship, this does not require a business license as long as you use your full name, in most states. Most people start their business this way because it is the easiest, cheapest and fastest way to start a business. You are essentially acting as a freelancer or independent contractor. So, you are responsible for paying your own taxes.

If you decide that you want to use a creative name for your business instead of your full name then you must obtain a business license and register your fictitious business name. You still want to check the zoning, industry and homeowner's association rules and regulations for your business. Even if you are using your full name and do not obtain a business license, your home may be located in a zone that does not allow the type of business you want to start. Every industry has its own requirements and regulations that you must comply with. And, if you live in a planned community the association has restrictions on the type of homebased businesses they allow to limit their liability and any inconvenience it may cause the other homeowners.

One of the main disadvantages of Sole Proprietorships is that you have unlimited liability, so if someone takes legal action against you all of your personal and business assets can be wiped out in an instant. For this reason, I recommend that you change your business from a Sole Proprietorship to some form of a corporation as soon as economically possible. Also, speak with legal and tax professionals to obtain the advice on which corporate structure would be best for your business.

3 How to Turn What You Know Into CASH

Now, that we've covered the basic business formula it is time to put on our thinking caps to come up with your MVP (minimum viable product) business. Which is the business you could start today with the skills you already have with a small investment. We all have potential but unfortunately most of us live our lives without ever realizing our potential. The skills you obtained from the jobs you've held, your hobbies and your talents is where the money is. Your talents are the things you do that people always compliment you on and say "you are so good at this I wish I could do that the way you do it", or something you always help people with and then say to yourself everyone should be able to do that so it is no big deal. Most people take their talents for granted.

There are no lengthy business plans required for this process. Because we are building a business we can start today to earn money, or extra money depending on your circumstances, and we are going to use this plan to make the money we need whenever we need it. If you decide to make it a full-time business then you can create a traditional business plan for future growth. But, for now we are just going to get started with what we know and refine our process and pivot along the way as needed so that we can reach our goals.

Also, remember the more service oriented the business the lower the start-up cost and the higher the ability to start **_today_**. For example, if you want to earn money raking leaves all you need is a rake and trash bags then you are in business and the cost is minimal. If you decide you want to earn money selling homemade soaps, then you have to buy the supplies, make the soaps, create a website, print business cards or flyers, the investment will be more expensive and you may not be able to start today because you do not have any products (soap) ready to sell.

Now, let us get started on coming up with ideas for your MVP (minimum viable product) business, that you are going to start today. You are going to make a list of your jobs, hobbies, duties, tasks, skills and MVP business ideas.

First make a list of all the different jobs that you have held, I'm sure it will be much shorter than mine, then list your hobbies. Next you are going to make a list of all the duties you performed in those jobs, and list all the tasks you do when engaging in your hobbies. After completing this, you are going to make a list of all of your transferable skills from your jobs and hobbies. Transferable skills are skills that can be used in other jobs or in a business that people will pay you to perform.

For example, your job position was an administrative assistant then your duties would include answering the telephone, taking messages, typing, written correspondence, scheduling appointments, customer service, account management, planning and organizing company meetings and events, writing checks, depositing payments, accepting payments, bookkeeping, sending and receiving packages, filing, coordinating with vendors, social media posts, website updates, editing and proof reading documents.

As we can see from this long list of duties, administrative assistants have a whole lot of transferrable money earning skills. A lot of people, companies and administrative assistants themselves take this job position for granted. And, most administrative assistants never realize their full potential and settle for making somewhere in the range of $9 - $15 per hour.

Now let's make a list of skills from the duties we listed. So, the transferable money earning skills would be: verbal and written communication, bookkeeping, proof reading, editing, data entry, planning, organizing, social media coordinator, website maintenance, shipping and receiving.

The final list in this example is for the possible MVP businesses. The MVP business ideas would be: transcription services, editing services, proof reading services, virtual assistant, social media assistant, website maintenance, event planning, meeting organizer,

For our next example, we are going to use the job position of a Maintenance Technician. The duties for this position include communication, plumbing, carpentry, electrical maintenance, painting, drywall, maintain and repair equipment, landscaping, HVAC, pest control, janitorial services, budget preparation, organization, leadership, management, planning and scheduling.

It is unfortunate how many people take the job position of a maintenance technician for granted too. As we can see from the list of duties, all of a maintenance technician's skills are transferable and they can earn money using any one of them as their MVP business.

If you are, or were, a manager that studied your industry and are considered a knowledgeable expert in your field then you can choose to become a consultant in the niche area of your field that you are most passionate about as your MVP business.

Using the list of MVP businesses created, you get to choose the one you are most passionate about and that you can start **_today_**. So now you really can do what you love to earn money.

Please take note of the fact that these MVP business ideas are based on the skills the administrative assistant, maintenance technician and manager **already have** and requires only a **small investment**. The old saying that *"it takes money to make money"* is correct, but it just doesn't take as much money as most people have been taught to believe.

The majority of these MVP businesses can be started with a free social media business page, business cards and or flyers. Since the social media business page is free you could purchase business cards or make flyers with a minimum investment of only $25 and you should start earning income in the first week. There is no need to mortgage the house or go out and get investors. And, you don't even have to pay for any expensive training courses to learn a new skill. So, essentially, we are turning what you already know into cash.

NOTES

4 Fact of Earning: It Takes WORK

So far you have learned the basic business formula, and the principle of turning what you know into cash. Now it is time to get down to the business of earning money with the MVP (minimum viable product) business you have chosen.

I'm sure there are some readers that are eager to find out how to make the $300 - $1,500 within 30-days, and others that are still skeptical and don't think it can be done. Earning $300 - $1,500 within 30-days isn't as difficult as some may think. The simple formula for this is:

Your Fee x Number of Clients = Your Earnings

If you obtain a minimum of ten clients in a month, 30-days, and charge each of those clients a minimum of $30 each, you have now earned $300 within 30-days. So, the math is very simple

$$\begin{array}{r}\$30\\ \underline{\times 10}\\ \$300\end{array}$$

There are approximately 20 working days in a month, which means you would be working with two to three clients a week to earn this amount of money. That is less than one client a day. Also, most business professionals charge an hourly fee for their services with a two-hour minimum requirement to hire them for their services.

If you obtain 20 clients in a month, 30-days, and charge each of those clients $37.50 with a two-hour minimum, for a total charge of $75, you have now earned $1,500 within 30-days. That amounts to working with one client each working day. So, the math looks like this

$$\begin{array}{r}\$75\\ \underline{\times 20}\\ \$1{,}500\end{array}$$

Now, if for some reason you do not feel anyone would pay you $30 for your services, then reduce the fee to $15 with a two-hour minimum requirement to hire you in order to earn $300 with ten clients or $600 with twenty clients within 30-days. As long as you provide a needed service and quality service for your clients, they will have no problem paying you your set fees.

    I know this for a fact, because back when I was in college I used to make cheesecakes from scratch and sell them for a minimum of $35 each to earn money, between steady jobs, and none of my clients ever complained. I even got catering jobs paying more than $1,500 each from clients based on how much they liked my cheesecakes. And, they didn't have any problem paying a college kid that amount of money because they **_valued_** my product and services. Some people may be wrestling with the issue of properly pricing for their services. This is also easier than you think. Call up three businesses that provide the same service as your MVP business and get quotes. You can use these quotes to set your fees as an average of the quotes or at 10% - 20% below your competitor's prices, just make sure you can deliver your services for that price and don't lose money on the transactions.

    You know how to price, now we have to focus on marketing. Everywhere you turn there is someone talking about how online marketing is the be all end all solution to getting customers and making sales. So, if this is true then every business owner that has a website and social media presence should have more customers than they can handle and their bank accounts should be overflowing with cash money.

However, if you ask some business owners they'll tell you that they have not made a single sale, received a single phone call, or generated a single lead from their website or social media presence. Depending upon your market and advertising budget an aggressive online marketing campaign could work well for a business. But, if your target market primarily uses pen, paper, fax and prefers to speak with business representatives by telephone or in person then this approach won't do you much good. Also, based on a study done by GE Capital Retail Bank, 81% of people look at products online before making a purchase and 88% of consumers make their final purchase IN STORE.

Since this is a MVP business for you to make money now we need to focus on low-cost fast response marketing not costly image advertising, and we don't want to wait several months to build a following to get clients. Our goal is to get you clients now and $300 - $1,500 within 30-days! So, your online presence should be limited to a free social media business page or website for now. If you decide to make this a permanent business then you can go all out, once you've earned the money, to pay for your desired online marketing services.

The most profitable businesses use both online and traditional offline marketing. Traditional marketing **_still works_**! Your traditional marketing will feed your online marketing, because people need to be able to FIND you. There are millions of businesses that are already online and have a social media presence, if your clients do not have the correct link to your exact website or social media page they could very easily wind up at a website or social media page that is *not* yours. Your flyers, business cards and any other traditional marketing media should always include your online information. By people and clients *seeing* this information repeatedly, they will be able to find you online, and it will feed your online marketing which could increase your return on investment, depending on your target market of course.

Now, because we want to earn $300 - $1,500 within 30-days we are going to focus on traditional marketing. As, the title of this chapter states, "It Takes Work". This is where we go out and get clients. We are going to employ old-school traditional offline marketing to reach our target market and get clients fast.

First tell everyone you know that you have started your MVP business. Then print up flyers, at least 200, and or business cards, whatever your budget will allow. Now it is time to hit the <u>actual</u> pavement. You are going to start walking, talking and handing out flyers to perspective clients everywhere. That means at the library, bookstore, your favorite restaurant, club meetings, free networking events, **<u>everywhere</u>**. Especially to people that you know from seeing or overhearing that they could use your services, just a tip these are the people you should give your flyers to first.

In the sales world, there is a basic rule of thumb that states it takes 20 cold prospects to get one sale. So, do not get discouraged if the first few people that you talk with don't become clients right away. The more prospects you meet the more sales you can make. Sales is a numbers game and you have to be persistent. And for those that think using the telephone to call prospects would be easier and more effective there is something called the Do Not Call list, which can make it difficult for you to call individuals, but you can call businesses all you want if they are your target market.

Keep in mind that you may need to change who and where you are marketing if you do not generate sales quickly. Because it usually means that you are in wrong target market. Let's say that your MVP business is a lawn mowing business and you're handing out flyers in a neighborhood where the planned community association maintains the lawns for their owners, then you are in the wrong market because a homeowner is not going pay you to perform a service that is included in their monthly association dues. Market your lawn care service in neighborhoods where people have to mow their lawns themselves or pay someone to do it for them. This is your target market people who will pay you so that they do not have to mow the lawn themselves or because you're cheaper than the company or person they currently use.

Here's another tip, your target market should need, want and be able to pay you for your services. If the people you are marketing to are not in this category then they are not your market or clients, at least not right now anyway. And just so you know, it takes an average of 6 years to become an "Overnight Success", according to RiseToTheTop.com. Once again, "It Takes Work"!

It takes work to earn money with a job. It takes work to earn money without a job. The simple fact is that if you need or want money, or in some cases you want more money, then you are going to have to work for it. One of my favorite quotes by T. Harv Eker, from the book SpeedWealth, is *"If you are going to work hard anyway, you may as well get rich... And the quicker the better"*.

5 Money Management Made Simple

We have covered how to earn it now we're going to cover how to keep it. Because as the old saying goes *"it's not how much you earn, it's how much you keep that matters"*.

Money management seems to be a missing skill for a lot of people these days. With approximately 75% of Americans living paycheck to paycheck, and that's at all levels of income. Which means, even people classified as rich live paycheck to paycheck too.

Money is something we use almost every day of our lives, but for some reason money management is not one of the core subjects taught in school. The majority of us would be much better off in life if it was taught in school. Because money is a tool that we use to pay for our living expenses. As Zig Ziglar has said *"money isn't everything but it's right up there with oxygen"*.

If you ask ten different people what the best way to manage your money is, you might just get ten different answers. Some people use complex money management systems and others use simple ones. Some people will tell you to pay off debt then save others will tell you to do the opposite. Other people will tell you to pay the debt with highest interest rate while still others say start with paying off your lowest debt. All these different money management methods are good if it *works* for you. If a program that you use doesn't work for you, no matter what type of program it is, stop using it and find one that does.

My money management program is simple:

- 10%   Charity
- 10%   Taxes
- 10%   Investments
- 10%   Savings
- 60%   Living Expenses and Enjoyment

This five account method is straight forward and simple because all of the money you earn in your MVP business is gross not net. If you have debt to payoff then you can reduce the savings amount to 5% and put the other 5% towards debt repayment. And for the record, I agree with the snowball method of paying off debt where you start making extra payments on the lowest debt while making minimum payments on all of your other debts, then applying that payment to your next debt, and continually progressing to the highest debt until you are debt free. This method allows you to see a form of accomplishment by eliminating debts one at a time and keeps you motivated to continue until you are debt free.

You should also look in to obtaining a business insurance policy to minimize your liability when transacting business. And, a life insurance policy to protect those you leave behind that depend on you for their livelihood. This is the responsible thing to do, sooner rather than later.

6 Money Mindset Paradigm Shift

It is time for a paradigm shift when it comes to your mind and money. There are a whole lot of people out here that believe money is the root of all evil. This is the most commonly incorrect quote of the Bible. The Bible does not say that money is the root of all evil, it says the love of money is the root of all evil.

Many people also believe that rich people don't pay their fair share in taxes due to the misrepresentation in the media. Yes, rich do people pay a lower tax rate than the average worker but they still pay more of than 50% of all the taxes collected by our government. Just check the government website to verify the statistics if you think I'm wrong. Some rich people pay more in taxes than most people make in a year. So in reality the tax percentage rate they pay may be lower but the actual dollar amount they pay is much higher. Rich people own the companies that create jobs. They also donate large amounts of money to charity. It is time for us all to understand that *money is just a tool, it is neither good nor bad, it is nothing more and nothing less.* Now let's stop hating on rich people, and being used by politicians for votes, and instead become a rich person so that we can do lots and lots of good with our millions.

Once we get over our negative attitude towards money and people that have money we can stop unconsciously sabotaging ourselves. Have you ever noticed a trend when it comes to your bank account and the amount of money in it? Like you get to a certain dollar amount in the account and you are happy for a while and everything is good. Then the before you know it the money is gone, you're back where you started and are hustling harder than ever to catchup the bills again. This cycle has probably repeated itself several times in your life.

And the cycle is probably still repeating itself in your life. This is you unconsciously sabotaging yourself when it comes to money. I speak from experience, because I have done it several times myself.

You are repelling money because of your mindset. If your mindset is that money is evil and people who have money are bad. Just think about it. What do you do when you know someone or something is bad? Do you run towards that person or thing? Or do you run away from it? Most of us try to stay as far away from bad people and things as we possibly can, because we don't want to go down with them. So, you are running away from money and you don't even know it.

It is time to start focusing on the good you can do with money. Believe that you deserve to have money and enjoy a good quality lifestyle. Develop a positive attitude towards money, the people that have money and all the good they do with money.

Be grateful for what you have already. Even if you don't think you have much. I'm sure you understand that things could always be worse, so you can at least be grateful that things aren't worse.

Create clear and concise goals for your life. Decide what type of life you want to live and the amount of money you want to earn. Choose the MVP business you would like to work so that you can earn that amount of money and live the lifestyle that you desire.

Deciding what you want is just the beginning. When you made the decision on the type of life and the amount of money you wanted that made you feel good. And many of the people reading this book will stop right there. Which means your decision was really nothing more than a dream. Some people want the luxury lifestyle and a boat load of money as long as they don't have to work for it. Reality check folks, as someone once said: *"the only place work comes before success is in the dictionary"*.

It is now time for you to **_commit_** to achieving your goals. A commitment means that you are actually going to do something. That means you're going to **_take action_**! This means that you are going to do at least one thing every single day, even if it's a baby step, towards achieving your goals.

Focus on your goals daily. Keep them in front of you everywhere. Write or print your goals on index cards, post-it notes, Avery business cards or even scraps of paper. Put these reminders everywhere: on the back of your cell phone, mirror in the bathroom, fridge, glove compartment, purse, wallet, on your computer. You can even make your goals your screen saver or password for the online places you visit frequently. As long as you can see your goals, you won't get to experience the out of sight out of mind syndrome and this will help keep you on track.

Just because your goals are everywhere and you've made a commitment it doesn't mean that things aren't going to happen. Acknowledge and accept it right now that life happens. Unfortunately, stuff happens. And when stuff happens don't get discouraged. Keep a positive mindset and remember to adopt the mantra "this too shall pass". During these times take the baby steps of planning what the first thing is that you're going to do when you get a minute to breath and get back on the road to achieving your goals. Visualize yourself achieving the goals you committed to. While visualizing yourself, take a minute and really feel the joy that you'll experience once your goal is achieved. Internalize your vision and use that for motivation to keep you going during the challenging times.

And believe me there will be challenges. Challenges like family and friends who mean well and are trying to protect you from the pain of failure being unsupportive and making negative comments or observations. Financial challenges like unexpected car repairs, medical bills or other bills. Things happen, we have to keep on moving because life doesn't come to a dead stop just because a challenge comes our way.

You can survive these challenges by loving your negative family members and friends from a distance. You call them a little less and you spend less time with them. When you hear yourself speaking or thinking negative things, shut it down immediately. Tell that negativity to go jump in the lake somewhere. Then ask yourself where is the proof that you cannot do it, and most times that proof doesn't exist. So that means you can! This will create a safe zone for you so that negativity doesn't distract you from achieving your goals. Read or listen to motivational books and join entrepreneur social groups, online and offline, so that you spend time with likeminded goal oriented people.

Creating a positive environment for yourself is essential to your success and achieving your goals. Also, make the decision and commit to managing your money properly. By taking these actions you will create a new money mindset paradigm, and finally stop repelling money and start attracting money.

7 Choosing to Earn By Temping

After reading the previous chapters you may feel that starting an MVP business is not for you. If it is because you need a regular paycheck to feel secure, or you would prefer to do something else that will hold you over until you find the job you want, then working for a temporary employment agency may be what you're looking for. You can bring in a regular paycheck and have the flexibility to search for your desired job. Also, a lot of employers are hiring through temporary service agencies so they can see if you are the right fit for their corporate culture and will be a good employee.

There are some people who actually work as a temporary employee for a living. They choose to work temporary jobs so they can control their time. As a temporary you get to decide when you are available to work and which job assignments you take. So, if you want to take the summers off, or go on a spur of the moment getaway, or need to take off because a family member is sick you can and without the fear that you may get fired for taking too many days off.

Remember you still have to work, even as a temporary employee. But if you get to a job location and you do not like the environment then you can contact the temporary employment agency inform them of the conditions and that you would like a different assignment beginning tomorrow or as soon as possible. Now, because assignments are not guaranteed, you should register with three or four different temporary employment agencies. By having multiple sources to receive job assignments from you can increase your chances for steady work.

You can do an online search for temporary employment agencies, temporary employment services, staffing agencies or employment agencies to obtain a list of the ones in your local area and look in a telephone book, if you can find one around. If you are relocating to a different area without a job, then add that area to you your online search. Some temporary employment agencies require you to submit your resume and complete your testing online before interviewing you in person, by telephone or live video. While others have you complete everything during an in-person interview. Regardless of which method is used, you will be required to take a few basic skills tests so they will know what job assignments you are qualified to do. If you are a good temporary worker the temporary agencies you work with will keep you working as much as they can, and you could even find yourself being hired as a permanent employee by one of your job assignment companies if you choose to accept the position.

8 The Earning Code Unlocked

You have learned how to earn money without a job as a temporary employee, freelancer, independent contractor, pop-up, spare-time or whenever you need money style business.

There are independent contractor home-based employment opportunities available also. Contracting with these type of companies, keeps you from having to go out and find clients on your own. It may take you longer than 30-days to start earning money because some of the companies require an interview, background check, testing, training and primarily communicate using email. Arise and LiveOps are two of the most widely known companies for this type of employment. You can start with these two and do an online search for others. This is not an endorsement or recommendation for either of these companies.

I also highly recommend picking up Woman's World magazine, of which I am an avid reader, and searching the $Ka-Ching! section for money earning opportunity ideas. The magazine First for Women also has home-based money earning opportunity articles, featured occasionally.

As we can see from reading this book, everyone has gifts and talents. We need to use our brain and ***think*** so we can become aware of what our gifts and talents are. Once we find them, we need to appreciate our gifts and talents. And understand that each person is unique, so we all have different gifts and talents. Then we need to ***think***, yes again you have to ***think,*** about ways you can use your unique gifts to help others in your MVP business which will in turn allow you to earn the money you need and or want so that you can have the lifestyle you desire.

In the closing of this book there are two things that I would like to remind people of a joke and a biblical story.

The joke:

What is the difference between a recession and a depression? It's a recession when your neighbor is out of work and it's a depression when you're out of work.

My summary of the biblical story (2Kings 4:1-7):

There was a widow with sons. She was afraid that her sons would be taken from her by her creditor and made slaves to work off the debts owed, since her husband died. She told the prophet that she had nothing in her house <u>but</u> some oil. The prophet told the woman to borrow pots and pour her oil into them. The oil filled every pot she had and could borrow. Then the prophet told her to go sell the oil so that she would earn enough money to pay off her debts and live prosperously with her sons.

The joke makes it clear that we need to work. And the biblical story makes it clear that we need to think because there are times when we feel that we have nothing, and we actually do have something <u>but</u> we've just been overlooking it, taking our talent for granted. Now there is no longer any excuse for you not to earn money for whatever reason you need or want it. All you have to do is just take action and work for it.

Make a commitment to take charge of your own personal economy. Use the information in these pages. And go <u>*EARN*</u> $300-$1,500, or more, within 30-days.

"*Live long, live well, think, work and prosper!*"

9 Recommended Resources

Lead the Field (Audio)

~Earl Nightingale

Secrets of the Millionaire Mind

~T. Harv Eker

SpeedWealth

~T. Harv Eker

How to be Rich

~J. Paul Getty

Multiple Streams of Income

~Robert Allen

Act Like A Success, Think Like A Success

~Steve Harvey

Jump

~Steve Harvey

Who Owns the Ice House?

~Clifton Taulbert and Gary Schoeniger

Ice House Entrepreneurship Program (Course)

info@elientrepreneur.com

Directing Your Destiny (Book and Course)

~Jennifer Grace

The Abundance Factor (Movie)

~Riley Dayne

10 Ideas, Worksheets, Examples And Samples

EXAMPLE

Jobs and Hobbies	**Duties and Tasks**
Administrative Assistant	*Answer telephone*
	Take messages
	Typing
	Correspondence
	Scheduling appointments
	Customer service
	Bookkeeping
	Filing
	Editing documents
	Proofreading documents
	Planning events
	Organizing meetings
	Vendor coordination
	Social media posts
	Website updates
	Shipping & receiving
	Account management

Jobs and Hobbies   **Duties and Tasks**

EXAMPLE

Skills	**MVP Business**
Verbal and written communication	*Editing services*
Bookkeeping	*Proofreading services*
Proofreading	*Virtual Assistant*
Editing	*Social media assistant*
Data entry	*Event planner*
Planning	*Meeting organizer*
Organizing	
Social media coordinator	
Website maintenance	
Shipping & receiving	

Skills   **MVP Business**

MVP Business Ideas

- Bookkeeping
- Business consulting
- Business support services
- Cleaning services
- Cooking lessons
- Desktop publishing
- Detailing service
- Dog walking
- Errand (Shopping) Service
- Event planning
- Foreign language lessons
- Graphic design
- Handyman services
- Interior decorating
- Image (Personal shopper) services
- Life coach
- Lawn mowing
- Moving services
- Pet sitting
- Photography
- Power washing
- Reminder service
- Scrapbooking
- Snow removal
- Tax preparation
- Tutoring
- Website maintenance
- Window washing
- Writing

BOOKKEEPING & TAXES

The following is a list of expenses you'll want to track so that you know how much you are spending and how much you're making. Doing this now will make preparing your taxes easier. You can set up a spreadsheet, use pen and paper or free app to track your payments and expenses.

    A simple way to track your expenses is to take a 9 x 12 envelope each month and put all the receipts for your business purchases, invoices and payments in it and on the last day of the month close it up write the month and year on it. If you prefer paperless tracking then you can update this information using a spreadsheet or free app monthly. To accept credit or debit card payments you may want to pick up a chip card reader like the Square, PayAnywhere or QuickBooks GoPayment. The next page lists expenses you may want to keep track of and depending on the MVP business you have chosen you may need to add more categories to this list.

EXPENSES

Advertising

Car and truck (actual or mileage)

Commissions and fees

Contract labor

Insurance (other than health)

Legal and professional services

Office expenses (phone, website, etc....)

Rent or lease (equipment, vehicles, etc....)

Repairs or maintenance

Supplies

Taxes and licenses

Travel, meals and entertainment

Other business expenses

Sample Flyers

DECLUTTER HELPER

Are your closets, garage, attic or other storage areas cluttered with JUNK?

If you are tired of looking at all your stuff,

And it's driving you Crazy then:

Call the

DECLUTTER HELPER!

We will help you declutter your storage areas…….

Professional Service provided around your schedule

Only **$30** *per hour*

LAWN MOWING MADE EASY

Need your lawn mowed?

Want affordable pricing?

Call today

We help make lawns look beautiful!

We offer free estimates, all season and one-time mowing

Starting at just **$30** *per hour*

SNOW REMOWAL SERVICE

Are you prepared for snow?

Want someone else to do the shoveling?

Call today

Snow usually arrives at the most inconvenient time

We provide all season and one-time removal plans

Starting at just $30 *per hour*

ORGANIZED SPACES

Is your stuff out of control?

Is your closet, garage, porch attic or other storage area overflowing with stuff and driving you crazy?

Call today

We will help you restore order to your home or office

And help you become sane again!

Only **$30** *per hour for the first 3-hours*

CLEANING SERVICES

Tired of washing your own windows, walls and floors?

Would you like someone else to do the cleaning for you?

Call today

We offer regular, deep and detail cleaning services

We provide weekly, monthly and one-time services

Starting at just **$30** *per hour for the first 3-hours*

ABOUT THE AUTHOR

Tashaya Singleton is an entrepreneur, insurance and training professional. With over 15 years of professional experience in business, training, insurance and financial services. She has trained employees of Fortune 500 Companies and a Global 100 company.

Her commitment to empowering individuals and businesses with the use of common sense perspectives that sometimes contradict conventional wisdom, as seen by the ideas put forth in this book, is unmatched.

Ms. Singleton is a former Board of Director of the Professional Insurance Agents Association of Virginia and DC. She also previously served as the Chairwoman for their Young Professionals Committee.

www.ingramcontent.com/pod-product-compliance
Lightning Source LLC
Chambersburg PA
CBHW061219180526
45170CB00003B/1065